THE ASD
WORKBOOK

of related interest

A Special Book About Me
A Book for Children Diagnosed with Asperger Syndrome
Josie Santomauro
Illustrated by Carla Marino
ISBN 978 1 84310 655 5

My Child Has Autism, Now What?
10 Steps to Get You Started
Susan Larson Kidd
ISBN 978 1 84905 841 4

Coach Yourself Through the Autism Spectrum
Ruth Knott Schroeder
Foreword by Linda Miller
ISBN 978 1 84905 801 8

Stand Up for Autism
A Boy, a Dog, and a Prescription for Laughter
Georgina J. Derbyshire
ISBN 978 1 84905 099 9

Hints and Tips for Helping Children with Autism Spectrum Disorders
Useful Strategies for Home, School, and the Community
Dion E. Betts and Nancy J. Patrick
ISBN 978 1 84310 896 2

PENNY KERSHAW

The ASD Workbook

UNDERSTANDING YOUR AUTISM SPECTRUM DISORDER

Jessica Kingsley Publishers
London and Philadelphia

First published in 2011
by Jessica Kingsley Publishers
116 Pentonville Road
London N1 9JB, UK
and
400 Market Street, Suite 400
Philadelphia, PA 19106, USA

www.jkp.com

Library of Congress Cataloging in Publication Data
A CIP catalog record for this book is available from the Library of Congress

British Library Cataloguing in Publication Data
A CIP catalogue record for this book is available from the British Library

ISBN 978 1 84905 195 8

Printed and bound in Great Britain

MIX
Paper from
responsible sources
FSC
www.fsc.org   FSC® C013604

ACKNOWLEDGEMENTS

Whenever anybody embarks on a long-term project it is inevitable that they will need the support of those closest to them and I therefore wish to thank Keith Blacktin for everything that he has done over the past few months to enable me to write this book.

This book has undoubtedly been enriched by Clare Jobling who, as a parent of a wonderful son with Asperger syndrome, has added her honest and valuable comments from a parent's perspective.

CONTENTS

ABOUT THE AUTHOR

Penny Kershaw is currently Autism Manager for a special school in East Sussex. She also provides training and support to staff, pupils with an autism spectrum disorder (ASD) and their families in mainstream and special schools in East Sussex.

She has extensive experience of working closely with a wide range of pupils who have ASDs.

Penny Kershaw has an MEd and she has undertaken various educational projects in the UK, Europe and the USA.

She has been motivated to write this book after realising that her talent for practical and straightforward advice has helped both children and their parents to understand more about the personal effects of ASDs.

Penny Kershaw has written widely on the subject of autism and communication needs and her work has been published by leading educational organisations. She is the co-author of *Inclusion in the Primary Classroom* and *Inclusion in the Secondary School*, which have been published by the National Autistic Society (NAS), UK.

PREFACE FOR PARENTS AND CARERS

Why this book was written

This book was written in response to the many parents and carers who have asked for advice about introducing a diagnosis of an autism spectrum disorder (ASD) to their child. The book aims to help children and adolescents with an ASD think through some of their difficulties. The material contained within this book is based on experience gained by working closely with parents, carers, children and adolescents who have all wanted to learn more about a diagnosis of an ASD. This experience led to the development of practical activities that have been used with children and adolescents to explore the personal significance of a diagnosis of an ASD. By consolidating this experience into one structured book it is my hope that young people and their parents, carers, children and adolescents will be provided with a positive understanding of a wide variety of ASDs.

Aims of this book

- To provide parents or carers with guidance on how to introduce an ASD diagnosis to their child.

- To help parents to develop a greater understanding of the effects of an ASD on their individual child.

- To allow parents, children and/or adolescents to develop a greater awareness of ASDs.

- To enable children and/or adolescents to understand how a diagnosis of an ASD affects them personally.

- To present information about a diagnosis of an ASD in a positive way.

Who is this book for?

This book is designed to be used by parents and carers who would like to introduce the diagnosis of an ASD to their child. Although this book has been written in general for children and/or adolescents from around 10 years old upwards, it is recommended that children or adolescents should have reached a level of understanding that will allow them to access the materials and activities that are contained within this book. You may find that your child is not ready to understand all of the content in this book straight away. In this case you could always leave some of the later chapters until you feel that your child has matured.

Parents should find that using this book with their child will stimulate discussion about their child's ASD. One of the aims of this book is that children or adolescents discover the personal and unique way in which an ASD affects them. Discussing the individual nature of ASDs should also lead parents to develop a deeper understanding of their own child's particular strengths and needs.

Additionally, this book may be useful for adults who are looking for a straightforward introduction to ASD. Adults with ASDs may also benefit from using the material in this book to explain their diagnosis to other adults or younger people. It is hoped that working through the materials in this book will enable people with ASDs to develop both their self-awareness and their awareness of other people.

Parents or professionals working with children or adolescents with ASDs may also find the ideas in this book helpful and interesting. These professionals, however, are strongly advised to seek the agreement of parents and carers before they introduce this book to their patients or pupils. Discussing a lifetime condition such as ASDs can have far-reaching implications for families, and it is therefore important that parents and carers have given their permission for this book to be used with their child.

When to use this book

This book is not intended to put pressure on parents to discuss ASDs with their child. The decision of whether or not to discuss ASDs with a child can be a difficult one to make and this decision should be an entirely personal one. This book is intended to be used when parents or carers and their child are all ready to talk about the personal effect of ASDs.

Parents whose children are already familiar with their diagnosis of ASD will also find this book useful. If your child already knows about his or her diagnosis then working through this book will enable you both to explore other issues (for example, about friendships) or to deepen your child's general understanding about the effects of ASDs.

Many parents find it difficult to judge if or when to explain a diagnosis of ASDs to their child. Some parents or carers see discussing ASDs with their child as an appropriate response to questions that are asked. Other parents or carers may decide to introduce the ASD diagnosis to their child before any such questions are asked.

There are five main reasons why parents or carers consider discussing an ASD diagnosis with their child:

- to provide more information once a child or adolescent has become aware of his or her ASD diagnosis

- to answer questions raised by your child about feeling 'different'

- to explain to family members or other people why your child behaves differently

- to offer explanations about certain situations that a child with an ASD may be experiencing difficulty with

- to introduce ASDs in order to raise self-awareness and prepare a child or adolescent for future events or challenges.

How to use this book

Structure of this book

This book is designed for parents and carers to introduce ASDs to their child. Parents and carers are advised to read through the book and familiarise themselves with all of the material before introducing this book to their child.

This book is arranged into ten distinct chapters. Chapter 1 is aimed specifically at parents and carers to provide them with guidance on using this book. Chapters 2 to 8 have activities that supplement the ideas set out in each chapter. Chapters 9 and 10 are for reference only.

The first eight chapters of the book have been written to guide you and your child systematically through the meaning of having an ASD and the effects that ASDs have on everyday situations. In this way the book has approached the introduction and explanation of ASDs in a systematic way. Parents and carers may feel that they need to vary the order in which the material is introduced to their child. However, it is strongly recommended that parents begin with Chapters 2 and 3 in that particular order as these two chapters provide the foundation for the rest of the material in this book. Parents with younger children might find that they need to leave some time for their child to mature before introducing the later chapters in this book.

Please bear in mind that the first reference you make to your child's ASD may make you feel awkward or uncomfortable. The following advice in this section should help you to be fully prepared in advance.

Before you start

Try to find a location in which you can begin working through this book that is as free as possible from potential distractions – for example, other siblings, a programme on television (particularly if this is a favourite programme for your child), loud and intrusive noise, etc.

Consider why you feel that it is important to discuss ASDs with your child at this particular time because this will determine when and how you decide to begin working through the ideas in this book (see the section on 'When to use this book' on p.15).

If your child has already asked questions or made comments about feeling different then use these questions or comments to introduce the material in this book and to start discussions.

If your child has not yet asked questions or made any comments, then decide in advance which words to use to start talking about ASDs. Some parents have used the following approaches to introducing a diagnosis of autism to their child:

- They have chosen a particular skill that their child has, and attributed the presence of this skill to having autism.

- Parents have referred to a specific incident that the child found difficult (e.g. when their child became upset because they were expected to share a favourite toy). Parents have then explained that the reason their child became so upset was because they are different and that difference is called autism.

- Some parents have introduced their child's diagnosis when they have returned home from diagnostic visits to clinics or hospitals.

Involving others

It is a good idea to let other people know (for example, family members or teachers) that you have begun talking about ASDs with your child. You may also want to consider how you would like them to respond to any questions or comments that your child might have about ASDs.

If your child has specific ASD support from teachers or staff at school you may like them to continue the discussion you have begun about having ASDs. If you feel that you would like this to happen, then it is advisable to discuss this and agree an approach in advance.

You may feel that it is appropriate to seek advice from a professional to see if they could help or support you when you introduce this book to your child, particularly when introducing the diagnosis. If you *do* decide to involve professionals then there will need to be close liaison between you and them.

It is extremely important that language used to explain ASDs is consistent in order to avoid any misunderstanding. Practical ways of ensuring consistency are achieved by the consistent use of the same words by all family members and all professionals involved; that is, once a diagnosis is introduced, the same terms to describe autism should be used throughout the workbook.

There are several words that may be used by professionals to describe or diagnose autism. Below is a list of these terms and a brief explanation of when each word may be used:

- ASD (autism spectrum disorder) – a more generic term that covers the full extent of skills or difficulties associated with autism.

- Asperger syndrome – very similar to high-functioning autism and based on the writings of Hans Asperger in the 1940s.

- Autism – can be used to refer to the condition of people who have delayed skills and display signs of autism based on the descriptions of Leo Kanner in the 1940s.

- High-functioning autism – used to describe the condition of people who show signs of autism but have average or above-average cognitive or language skills.

Also, try to make sure that the explanation of ASDs and the material in this book is always approached in a positive way.

Timing

The initial mention of ASDs will probably need sensitive handling so it is important to choose a time when your child is less likely to be tired, anxious or involved with one of his or her favourite activities.

It is recommended that you decide upon a time to discuss ASDs in advance and then plan or timetable this discussion into the day. Your child may need some notice, or to be given a set time to talk to you about ASDs. You should probably use whatever arrangement you have already for introducing new activities or signalling for a change in activities, so that the initial discussion can be easily fitted into your family routine.

However, do be prepared to be 'caught out' as some parents have found that their child has asked questions about ASDs at inconvenient times. When your child has already had a diagnosis of ASD it would be worthwhile preparing a simple answer to any initial questions that you can give straight away, before then introducing the material in this book.

Try to establish a realistic timescale for using this book with your child. It is a good idea to work through it systematically rather than beginning the book and then having a long break between sections.

There is no time limit on how long this book takes to complete, but it is advisable to have regular set times to talk about the material and complete the activities. Roughly one section per week is a useful guide.

Alternatively, if your child is already familiar with their diagnosis then you may wish to use some of the chapters in this book to discuss other issues as and when they arise – for example, Chapter 4 about the family.

Remember that your first discussion of ASDs with your child may have a big effect on them. Your child may ask lots of questions, experience a sense of relief, or initially find learning about his or her diagnosis difficult. Your child may need time to reflect on the fact that he or she has an ASD. Ideally, this book should be approached one section at a time so that there is time to consider and talk fully about the ideas presented.

If your child is particularly eager to learn more about his or her ASD and you, as a parent or carer, can establish the right space and environment to work through this book then it is recommended that the *absolute maximum* number of sections to work through is one section per day. It is important to point out here that the problem is not necessarily the amount of time that it will take to work through this book but the ability to create sufficient time and the right environment to stimulate positive discussion. Finally, you might want to plan to revisit some of the material in this book to consolidate understanding or to answer any specific questions that your child asks. On the following page you will find a checklist that will help to guide you, or any professional involved, through the process of introducing a diagnosis of autism.

At the end of this book there is a progress chart that you and your child can fill in together so that you can see the sections that are finished and which sections need to be completed.

Introducing ASDs: Checklist

☐ Decide how long you want to discuss ASDs for.

☐ Draw up a rough timetable to work through this book, chapter by chapter.

☐ Decide when the discussion about ASDs will take place.

☐ Decide where the discussion about ASDs will take place.

☐ Decide who will lead the discussion about ASDs.

☐ Decide who else might be involved, e.g. professionals.

☐ If others, e.g. professionals, *are* involved decide on their specific role.

☐ Decide which terms to use, e.g. autism, ASDs, Asperger syndrome, etc.

☐ Decide which strengths you will highlight, e.g. computers, drawing, etc. (Try to think of the strengths that your child will identify with).

☐ Decide which difficulties you will highlight, e.g. sharing, listening, etc.

☐ Decide which phrases to use to introduce ASDs.

Chapter **1**

INTRODUCTION

Learning about autism spectrum disorders (ASDs)

Most children or adolescents with ASDs find that learning more about ASDs helps them to better understand their own experiences and the behaviour and reactions of others.

Learning more about having an ASD is valuable because:

- it can provide explanations for situations that you may have found hard to understand

- adults with an ASD have sometimes described feeling guilty or bad about their behaviour at times before they found out that they had an ASD

- other people often respond in a more positive way to a person with an ASD diagnosis if it is explained to them

- many people develop relaxed friendships with others who have the same or similar ASD diagnosis

- understanding how an ASD affects each individual makes it easier for you to develop your own ways to cope with difficult situations.

Learning more about having an ASD can have its drawbacks too.

- To begin with, it may be hard to accept that you are 'different'.

- It can feel unfair to have an ASD.

- It can be hard to cope with the fact that, to date, there is no known cause or cure for an ASD.

These drawbacks do not mean that you should avoid discussing the fact that you have an ASD. The major aim of this book is to give you the confidence to talk about and learn more about ASDs and how having ASD affects you. It is best not to go through all of this workbook at once – try to go through one chapter at a time and remember to ask your parent or carer to talk to you about what you have read or written in this workbook.

Chapter **2**

WHAT IS AN ASD?

What does the diagnosis mean?

Having a diagnosis of autism or Asperger syndrome (an autism spectrum diagnosis or ASD) means that you think, or process information, in a different way from people without that particular diagnosis. People who don't have an ASD generally think in similar ways whereas people with an ASD think in a way that is sometimes unusual or difficult for other people to understand. You may also have had problems dealing with other people or with friendships because of the differences between people who don't have an ASD and people with an ASD.

Some people are more affected by their ASD than others and it is very important to realise that an ASD is often described as a 'spectrum' or 'continuum'. A spectrum or continuum means that there are lots of different ways that an ASD affects each person with that diagnosis. An ASD covers a wide range of ways that people think, feel or behave. Every person with an ASD will have different problems and different strengths. This makes an ASD complicated but also very interesting. However, all people with an ASD share a common set of difficulties.

A diagnosis of an ASD means that you have a different thinking style and may also have difficulty with some or all of the following:

- social interaction
- communication
- social imagination

- dealing with sensory information like noise or smells
- changing the way you think about things, e.g. accepting changes in routines
- coping with different situations or sudden changes in your routine.

You may not be familiar with some of these words so they are all explained below.

Social interaction

Social interaction means being in the same room or place as other people and responding to what they do. Examples of difficulties with social interaction are:

Proximity – knowing how near or far away to stand from other people.

Body language – understanding what people mean by looking at the way their bodies move.

Sharing – taking turns or using objects with other people.

Facial expressions – what people say without using words. For example, a smile is actually saying you are happy and a frown could mean that someone is cross.

Attention – knowing when and how to listen to somebody or how to let somebody know that you want them to listen to you.

Making friends – you might find it hard to make new friends or have difficulty keeping friendships that you have made.

Social communication

This is how people let each other know their thoughts and feelings.

Reciprocity – communication involves two or more people, who both listen to each other and both respond to each other.

Intonation – loudness or quietness, and the tone, of the voice gives extra meaning to what is being said.

Humour or idioms – people use humour every day when they talk. Humour is not serious or correct and is usually not meant to be taken literally. People may also use idioms that are expressions that really mean something totally different, for example, 'It's raining cats and dogs' (which means it is raining a lot).

Other people's emotions – people can appear to be insensitive if they have not recognised how someone else is feeling.

Conversations – in a conversation people are expected to:

- join in a conversation at the right time; this includes taking turns to talk, listening and answering questions

- talk about the same subject as each other

- let the listener know if they want to change the subject being talked about

- finish the conversation in a polite way.

Shared knowledge – this means the sort of things that most people already know about a situation, for example, a bus driver will already know where his bus is travelling to. Having shared knowledge stops people from 'stating the obvious', which means telling people what they already know.

Social imagination

Social imagination allows us to understand other people's behaviour and also to understand what they are likely to do. Social imagination will also help us to make sense of other people's ideas, and to imagine what it is like to do things that we do not do every day. Difficulties with social imagination mean that people with autism find it hard to:

- understand other people's thoughts, feelings and actions

- predict, or have a good guess at, what will happen next, or what *could* happen next

- understand what is dangerous – e.g. running on to a busy road

- join in with imaginative play and activities that involve pretending

- work out what to do in new or unfamiliar situations.

Do not confuse difficulties with social imagination with a *lack* of imagination. Many people with ASDs are very creative and may be, for example, artists, musicians or writers.

Activity 1: Your differences

Talk to the adult or friend that you are working with about how you may be different. List five things that are different about you compared with your friends or family.

I am different to my friends and family because:

1. . . . .

2. . . . .

3. . . . .

4. . . . .

5. . . . .

Activity 2: Your difficulties

List five things that you find difficult. If you need to, then read through this chapter again for some ideas of things that people with an ASD might find hard.

I find these things difficult:

1. . . . .

2. . . . .

3. . . . .

4. . . . .

5. . . . .

Activity 3: What I like doing

List five things that you like to do. You can ask your parents or another adult if you need some help.

I like doing these things:

1. . . . .

2. . . . .

3. . . . .

4. . . . .

5. . . . .

Why have I got this diagnosis?

A diagnosis is a type of name or label. Labels help us to group together things that are similar. Grouping similar things together helps us to organise our understanding. The name or label 'cat' means that we know a cat is a furry animal with four legs and a tail. Our own names tell others who we are. We need names and labels to understand what things are or what things mean.

The names or labels 'autism', 'Asperger syndrome' or an 'autism spectrum disorder' (an ASD) are a quick way to explain how you may be different or what things you may find easy or hard. A diagnosis of an ASD helps your family, teachers, employers and other people know that you are different and helps them to understand what you do that may look confusing to them. A specialist who knows a lot about autism can give people a diagnosis of an ASD.

If you already have a diagnosis of an ASD this means that at some point in your life you have been to see a specialist (or a team of specialists) who have watched you and talked to your parents. The specialist (or team of specialists) has recognised that your particular way of thinking or processing information fits the descriptions of an ASD according to the information that has already been written by doctors.

There are also lots of different types of ASD assessments for people of different ages. These assessments are also used by specialists to help them understand more fully if you have an ASD and the particular difficulties that you may face.

People can be diagnosed with an ASD at any age. When a specialist is thinking about a diagnosis of an ASD they will try to find out if you have always had all, or most of, the difficulties listed in their assessments. If you are an adult they may ask you questions about your friendships or interests. If you are a child they will ask your parents questions about what you were like when you were growing up. You may have been asked to talk to some specialists or play with some toys while the specialist listened to what you said or watched how you played.

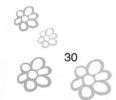

The specialist looks carefully at:

- how you talk to other people

- what you do in a new situation

- how you understand faces or emotions

- what interests or hobbies you have.

Activity 4: You and ASD

Below is a list of things that people with an ASD have said about how their diagnosis affects them.

Which of these sentences about an ASD apply to you?

Put a tick ☑ in the box if you agree, or a cross ☒ in the box if you don't.

Talking to people and being with people

☐ I like time on my own and prefer to do things on my own.

☐ I tell the truth and I get annoyed when other people tell lies.

☐ I don't always want to look at people when they talk to me.

☐ Sometimes people get cross with me and I don't understand why.

☐ Understanding or remembering words can be hard.

☐ I don't always know how people feel by looking at their faces.

☐ I'm good with numbers or pictures but not so good with words.

☐ Sometimes I don't think other people's jokes are funny.

☐ I feel awkward joining in with my family or with groups of people.

☐ I don't know what to do or say when I talk to people.

☐ Too many people in rooms or places make me feel tense.

☐ I feel more relaxed with other people who have autism or Asperger syndrome.

☐ Some people tell me not to worry but they don't always help me.

Sensory needs

☐ Some things really bother me that other people don't care about, like the smell of a banana or how furniture is arranged.

☐ I am sensitive to some things; I have sensory difficulties like problems with noise or fabrics.

☐ I don't like going to the hairdresser's.

☐ I find some foods difficult to chew or swallow.

☐ I don't always like to be hugged or touched.

Flexible thinking

☐ I notice things that other people don't, like the pattern on a carpet.

☐ I prefer familiar things to new ones.

☐ I don't always enjoy going to new places.

☐ Some people don't share my interests.

☐ I like to find patterns or systems and enjoy arranging things.

☐ I feel uncomfortable if I can't predict what will happen next in situations.

☐ Sudden changes are hard for me to cope with if I'm not prepared.

☐ I think differently to most people and have my own way of doing things.

☐ I like to learn facts and read information books.

☐ When I am at school or at work I prefer to finish activities without being interrupted.

☐ I am very good at working with computers or playing computer games.

☐ Sharing can be hard for me.

Think about the checklist that you have just done for Activity 4.

How many ticks did you have? Write your answer here . . . .

How many crosses did you have? Write your answer here . . . .

Did you find out anything new about yourself? Ask your parent or an adult to help you to write five things that you learned about yourself below.

I learned these new things about myself:

1. . . . .

2. . . . .

3. . . . .

4. . . . .

5. . . . .

What to do next

1. Make sure that you know what having a diagnosis of an ASD means.

2. Talk to the adult or a friend who you are working with about any of the words in Chapter 2 that you don't understand.

3. If there are any parts of this chapter that you have found difficult to complete then ask the adult or friend who you are working with to help you with these.

4. Remember that when people understand what you find difficult or what you dislike then they can help you.

5. Try to find out about other people who have an ASD – there are some books and websites in Chapter 9 that will help you to do this.

Chapter **3**

UNDERSTANDING YOUR DIFFERENCES

If you have an ASD you might feel different to most people that you meet. Other people might seem strange or angry, or might make you feel confused. It is important to understand that:

- Your differences have a name and that name is an ASD.

- ASDs are described in lots of books and on the internet.

- The information about an ASD can help you and others understand more about your strengths and difficulties.

- There is really no such thing as a completely normal person! You don't have to feel bad about having an ASD – some people see it as a gift.

- Everybody is actually very different. We all like different things and want different things from our lives.

People with an ASD are different

Here is a list of the main differences that people with an ASD have:

1. *Interests* – your interests may not be the same as other people that you meet.

2. *Systems* – you will probably be better at and more interested in systems or patterns of things than being with people.

3. *Social skills* – sometimes you will feel awkward in social situations – being with other people and enjoying their company may not be easy for you.

4. *Communication* – you may find it hard to explain things or to understand what people say to you, especially if they give you lots of information at once.

5. *Sensory sensitivity* – things like

    o noise

    o fabric

    o the taste of some food

    o lights

    o smells

    could be uncomfortable for you – this is called 'sensory sensitivity'.

You may also find that you do not notice some sensory things as much as other people – for example, you may not feel when your body gets very cold or very hot.

These differences are not bad but they can cause you some problems that you might need help with. It is important for you to understand that these problems will probably be because some people don't understand that you have an ASD or what an ASD means.

People with an ASD sometimes have problems

Read through this list and think about any of the things in the list that apply to you. Ask a parent or an adult to help you.

1. *Interests:*

    o You may find it hard to make friends who don't have the same interests as you.

    o You find it hard to understand why other people don't like the same things as you.

- Some people may think you are strange.

- You could have difficulty concentrating on other things if you are thinking about your interests.

2. *Systems:*

- Routines could be more important to you than to other people.

- Other people may not understand that you need routines.

- Other people may not understand that you are more interested in systems than team games or other people.

- You may find changes or new things hard and other people may not understand why you are anxious.

3. *Social skills:*

- You may try to talk to people but you may say the wrong things to people and upset them.

- People could think that you are rude or badly behaved.

- You may not always be able to join in with groups when other people expect you to.

- It is important to understand that most children learn how to talk to and to be with people when they are little. Because you have an ASD this means that you learn different things in different ways and you may not have learned how to talk to and to be with people. Learning how to talk to or be with people is called 'social skills'.

4. *Communication:*

- People show a lot of things by the way they move parts of their body – this is called 'body language'. You could find body language hard to understand (e.g. the way people's faces look when they are talking) and so you may not understand what they mean.

- You could also find it hard to understand that the type of voice people use means different things. Sometimes people say strange things and they don't really mean what they say, e.g. 'Pull your socks up' really means 'Try harder'.

o   You might have to learn what these strange sayings (idioms) really mean. Sometimes people also say things that mean the opposite. This is called 'sarcasm', e.g. saying that something is good but really meaning that something is bad.

o   People who do not have an ASD usually learn how to communicate, learn how to read body language and understand when people don't really mean what they say naturally – that means without trying.

o   Because most people learn how to communicate without special lessons, they may think that you are being deliberately rude if you make mistakes

5.   *Sensory sensitivity:*

o   This may affect you in different ways:

Sensory things (things that you touch, taste, see, smell or hear) could be painful for you or make it very difficult for you to do things like sit at a table and eat with other people. People may not understand why it is painful for you or very difficult for you to do some things because people who do not have an ASD are not usually affected by sensory input.

If you find it hard to feel sensory things then you might hurt yourself. For example if you found it hard to know how hot the water in a bath is then you might get in a very hot bath and burn yourself in the hot water.

Understanding more about an ASD – the difficulties and the good things

Activity 5: Your interests

What are your three favourite interests? List them here.

My three favourite interests are:

1. ....

   ....

2. ....

   ....

3. ....

   ....

What are the things that people are interested in at your school or work? List them here.

The things that other people are interested in at my school or work are:

1. ....

   ....

2. ....

   ....

3. ....

   ....

What are the interests of people in your family? List them here.

My family are interested in these things:

1. ....

....

2. ....

....

3. ....

....

The lists that you have made probably show you that people all have various interests and that your interests may be different to other people's.

Are there any interests that you and your family can share? List them here.

Our shared interests are:

1. ....

....

2. ....

....

3. ....

....

42

Activity 6: Managing your interests

Do you find it hard to limit your interests or stop thinking about them when other people tell you to? If so, you need to think about ways to make this easier for yourself. These ideas might help you.

Put a tick ☑ in the box if you agree or a cross ☒ in the box if you don't.

☐ Having a warning so that you can prepare to finish thinking about your interests.

☐ Having a set time in the day when you can think about your interests.

☐ Being able to ask for a fixed time at home, school or work to think about your interests.

☐ Keeping objects that you like in the same place so that you know where they are and you don't have to worry about them.

☐ Using your interests at school or work, e.g. joining a model train collectors' club or using the computer to help you with your work.

Activity 7: Your interests — problems and benefits

List three problems that you might have with your interests.

What problems do my interests cause?

1. ....

   ....

2. ....

   ....

3. ....

   ....

Now list three good things (called 'benefits') about your interests.

The benefits of my interests are:

1. ....

   ....

2. ....

   ....

3. ....

   ....

Liking systems, patterns or routines

A system is a way of organising information or parts of a machine. Systems are everywhere in our lives. A traffic light is a system to control how cars cross roads. A train timetable is a system that shows when and where trains go. Computers use lots of systems so that they can process or make use of information like games or the internet. If you have an ASD you may like thinking about systems more than other people.

A pattern is a way that something is written down or arranged. Patterns are predictable; that means that they always happen in the same way. Like numbers they always stay in the same order. People with an ASD may enjoy patterns because they are clear and sometimes the world can seem confusing.

A routine is a way of doing things in the same order. Everybody uses some routines to help them, like doing some things on the same day or at the same time each day. If you have an ASD you might find that you need routines to help you feel safe and comfortable and find it hard if these routines are interrupted.

Activity 8: Systems, patterns and routines

What systems do you like? For example, computer systems.

I like these systems: ....

....

Are there any patterns that you like? For example, number patterns.

I like these patterns: ....

....

Do you have any routines? For example, when you get up in the morning.

I have these routines:

....

....

....

....

....

....

Put a tick ☑ in the box if you agree or a cross ☒ in the box if you don't.

☐   I feel upset if I don't have systems, patterns or a routine.

☐   I feel upset if my systems, patterns or routines are changed suddenly.

☐   I feel upset if I cannot follow my systems or patterns, or if my routines are changed suddenly.

Now think of three examples of times when it is difficult to follow systems, patterns or routines (for example, when there is a lot of noise).

It is hard for me to follow systems, patterns or routines when:

1. . . . .

    . . . .

2. . . . .

    . . . .

3. . . . .

    . . . .

List three examples when systems, patterns or routines help you.

Systems, patterns or routines help me because:

1. . . . .

    . . . .

2. . . . .

    . . . .

3. . . . .

    . . . .

Social skills

People who don't have an ASD usually learn social skills quite easily. People who don't have an ASD often enjoy socialising – that means being with friends or being with lots of other people. People who don't have an ASD may not understand that you do not always want to socialise, or that you find social situations uncomfortable.

Activity 9: Social skills

Put a tick ☑ in the box if you agree or a cross ☒ in the box if you don't.

☐   I find it hard to talk to people that I don't know.

☐   I find it hard to join in with a group.

☐   I like to spend time on my own.

☐   Crowded places make me feel uncomfortable.

☐   I like it when people help me with social situations.

List three examples of when you find socialising difficult.

Socialising is difficult for me when:

1. ....

   ....

2. ....

   ....

3. ....

   ....

People with an ASD can develop or learn good social skills. These might include having good manners, like always saying 'please' and 'thank you' or waiting in line for a turn. Now you need to think about your social skills strengths.

Put a tick ☑ in the box if you agree or a cross ☒ in the box if you don't.

☐   I remember to say please and thank you.

☐   I can wait until it is my turn.

☐   I have good table manners – e.g. I use a knife and fork properly and don't talk if I have food in my mouth.

☐   I can be in crowds of people and not feel uncomfortable.

☐   I like going to new places when I know what will happen.

Are there any other social situations that you do well in?

Put a tick ☑ in the box if you can or a cross ☒ in the box if you need to learn how to do this.

☐   Sit quietly and wait, e.g. at the doctor's or dentist.

☐   Let other people look at the things that I like, e.g. my special interests.

☐   Stand the right distance away from people.

☐   Try to look at people to show them that I am listening to them.

☐   Wait in a queue without pushing in.

☐   Join in with a group without looking like I am being rude.

☐   Leave a group without looking like I am being rude.

☐   Work well or cooperate with somebody else to do something.

☐   Remember to cover my mouth every time that I cough.

☐   Remember not to point at people even if I am talking about them.

Communication

Lots of people find it hard to communicate – not just people with an ASD. Communication is important. Good communication means that we can explain to other people what we mean and understand what other people are telling us.

Activity 10: Communication

Put a tick ☑ in the box if you agree or a cross ☒ in the box if you don't.

☐ It is hard for me to understand how people feel just by looking at their faces.

☐ I find it hard to understand lots of spoken instructions.

☐ People don't always understand what I mean.

☐ Sometimes people laugh at me or get annoyed with me and I don't know why.

☐ I find it hard to listen to other people for a long time.

Is there anything else about communication that you find hard? Write it here:

. . . .

. . . .

. . . .

. . . .

An ASD means that you have a set of recognised difficulties but you also have lots of strengths. Difficulties and strengths are both part of having an ASD. Below is a list of strengths that you may have.

Put a tick ☑ in the box if you agree or a cross ☒ in the box if you don't.

☐ I enjoy talking about my interests.

☐ I say hello to people when I meet them.

☐ I like talking to people that I know well.

☐ I can explain to people about things that I do well, e.g. the computer.

☐ I am good at joining in with groups of people when I know what to do.

Do you have any other communication strengths? Try to think of three communication strengths that you have.

Put a tick ☑ in the box if you agree or a cross ☒ in the box if you don't.

I have these communication strengths:

☐ I can make a telephone call.

☐ I can give someone directions.

☐ I can ask for directions.

☐ I can take turns in a conversation.

☐ I can explain to people if I don't understand what they are saying.

☐ I can ask a friend to help me at school or work.

☐ I can listen to people without interrupting them.

☐ I can remember a message and give the message to the right person.

☐ I can ask other people questions if I need to.

☐ I can use people's names that I know to get their attention.

Sensory sensitivity

Everybody uses their five senses all the time. We hear, feel or touch, taste, smell and see things. The five senses are important because we use them to experience our world – this is called 'sensory information' or 'sensory processing'. Sometimes people with an ASD feel sensory information differently – usually this means that they experience sensory information more strongly than people without an ASD. This is called '*hyper*-sensitivity'. Other people with an ASD may not experience sensory information very much at all – this is called '*hypo*-sensitivity'.

Sounds may seem much louder than they do for someone who does not have an ASD, textures or surfaces of things can feel rougher, tastes of food may be stronger, smells can be more powerful and lights may hurt your eyes. However, some people with an ASD may actually be drawn to some sensory experiences, for example, some smells or the feel of some materials.

Activity 11: Sensory issues

Below is a list of the five senses. List something that you like and something that you don't like for each one.

Sound/noise

I like this noise: . . . .

. . . .

I don't like this noise: . . . .

. . . .

Touch

I like the feel of . . . .

. . . .

I don't like the feel of . . . .

. . . .

Taste/food and drink

I like the taste of . . . .

. . . .

I don't like the taste of . . . .

. . . .

Smells

I like the smell of ....

....

I don't like the smell of ....

....

Sight

I like looking at or seeing ....

....

I don't like looking at or seeing ....

....

What to do next

1. With a friend or adult, make sure you understand the main points of this chapter called Understanding Your Differences. The main points are:

    o   your interests

    o   systems, patterns and routines

    o   social skills

    o   communication

    o   sensory sensitivity.

2. Tell your friend or adult working with you if you don't understand anything about the main points and ask them to explain it to you.

3. Ask your friend or adult questions if you need to – remember to ask only questions about:

    o   an ASD

    o   your interests

    o   systems, patterns and routines

    o   social skills

    o   communication

    o   sensory sensitivity.

4. Along with a friend or adult, choose five of your strengths from this chapter – you will need this information later in this workbook.

5. Along with a friend or adult, choose five of your difficulties from this chapter – you will need this information later in this workbook.

6. When you have finished, tick the sections in your progress chart.

Chapter **4**

PEOPLE YOU LIVE WITH

Why is home life important?

Most people in the world have a home. A home is made up of a building with different people living in that building. The people who live at home with you are called your family. Every family and every home is different.

There are lots of different types of families. Your immediate family is a group of people who are related to each other – that means that they share the same mother, father, brothers or sisters. An 'extended family' may also include other relatives like cousins, aunties, uncles and grandparents.

Some of you may have been adopted. Adopted children are children whose family have not been able to bring them up and so their family has changed by law; they are now part of a new family. Adopted children live with and grow up with their new family as if they were born into their new family. The diagram on the next page explains different people found in families and how they are related.

Some families include your mum or dad, brothers or sisters. Some families include carers (adults looking after children); carers may look after children in a children's home. Not everyone is able to live with their immediate family. There will be good reasons why some people who live with people other than their immediate family. There are also families called 'foster families'. Foster families look after children who are not actually related to them but who they care about in just the same way. Foster brothers or sisters may live in a home with you but you might not have the same mum or dad. Foster families may look after children for a short length of time or for a long time.

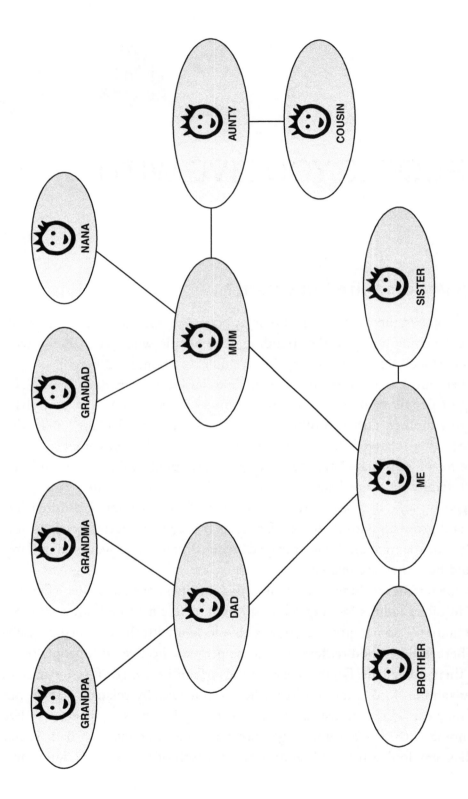

Example of a family map: this shows different people that may be in a family

Some people who have an ASD have difficulty knowing why their parents or carers get cross or upset with them because of the things that they say or do to other people in the family home. Some people with an ASD also find it hard to understand why home life is important. This chapter will help you to understand why home life is important and learn more about problems that you and your family or carers might have because of an ASD. Later in the chapter there are some ideas to help you and everybody else living in your home to understand each other.

You are very important to your family. Home life and the people that you live with are important to you because:

- they are the people who support and care for you

- there are people who love you in your family. Having people who love you means that these people will always help you and protect you

- people in your family will guide you. That means that they will show you what to do and help you to learn right from wrong

- you may be related to your family, which means that your mother and father might have actually made you and, because of that, they will feel close to you

- your family will have people in it that you can trust. 'Trust' means that people will do what they say: they always try to keep promises and always do the best thing for you. Being able to trust people means that you will get help and support when you need it.

Problems you might have in a family

Your family will be interested in what you think and what you feel. However, you may find that you have problems in your family. There are some common problems that people with an ASD have with their families. Usually these problems are caused by things that your family just expect you to do without telling you.

Families give you a lot of things. These things may be objects like computers, food, warmth, somewhere to live or other things like time or help. Because families give you a lot of things they can also expect things back in return; this is called 'having expectations'. Family expectations happen even if you haven't actually asked anybody in your family for things like time, money or help. It is important for you to understand about the expectations that your family have because the people in your family might get upset or angry if you don't follow these expectations.

Here is a list of some things that people living together at home expect from each other – it is possible that you might not be aware of some of these things. You may be expected to:

- like the people in your family the best – that means liking them better than things like the computer or other people

- do things together with other people in your family

- share your things with a brother or sister

- look after other people in your family when you go out, e.g. to work or school

- not take people's things without their permission

- give affection like hugs and kisses

- be interested in the people in your family, like feeling sad if people in your family are hurt or upset

- say sorry if you do something to hurt or upset someone that you live with

- get along, which means not arguing too much with people in your family

- talk to your family about what you are doing or things that you have done at work or school

- explain your problems and let your family help you with them

- not say unkind things to, or about, other people in your family.

Difficulties that your family might have with your ASD

If you have an ASD then you might find that fitting into a family could be difficult for you because sometimes you and your family members may not understand each other. Your family will want to feel close to you. Sometimes you might not feel comfortable with your family. There are things that your family will need you to do, like keep your bedroom tidy or help with the washing up, and if you can't do these things or if you don't understand these things, then this might be difficult for your family. Here is a list of things that your family might find hard.

People in your family might find it hard if:

- they do not know how you are feeling

- they do not know what you are thinking

- they do not know what you like

- they do not know what you *don't* like

- they cannot talk to you about work or school

- they cannot enjoy doing things with you like talking or playing games

- they don't understand what you are upset about

- they don't understand why your interests or routines are important to you

- you say unkind things to people, even if you don't understand how upsetting this can be

- you don't show any interest in people in your family, e.g. how they are feeling.

Activity 12: Family talk

Choose one person in your family who you could try to talk to every day. Use the list below to help you.

Every day I will try to tell someone in my family:

1. one thing that I have done at home

2. one thing that I have done at school

3. one thing that I liked doing at home, school or work and why I liked it

4. one thing that I didn't like doing at home, school or work and why I didn't like it

5. one thing that made me feel happy, sad, angry, upset or frightened and why it made me feel that way.

Also, remember to ask the person what he or she has done today.

If you are able to do this every day then you will find that you will get help if you need it, and the person that you talk to will be very pleased that you have talked to them. It will make them feel special and wanted.

Activity 13: Family difficulties

You may need help from your parent or an adult to fill in this section of the workbook.

List five things that you and your family may find difficult because you have a diagnosis of an ASD.

My family might find it difficult when I:

1. ....

   ....

2. ....

   ....

3. ....

   ....

4. ....

   ....

5. ....

   ....

Activity 14: House rules

Now list five rules that you think you and your family could have in your house or home. These rules should make the five family difficulties easier to cope with. Here is an example of house rules:

1. Always say hello to people in your family when you first see them.

2. Always say goodbye to people in your family before you leave them.

3. Nobody takes or moves someone's things without asking first.

4. My family will not shout at me if I do something wrong – they will explain.

5. I will try not to shout at people in my family if they do something wrong – I will explain what the problem is calmly.

Your family rules

Remember to talk to someone in your family first and agree these rules with them. You could talk to your mother, father, brother or sister. These rules are for you and your family.

My family has these rules:

1. ....
    ....

2. ....
    ....

3. ....
    ....

4. ....

....

5. ....

....

What to do next

1. Make sure that you understand who is in your family and why they are important.

2. Learn about some things that other people in your family like doing.

3. Try to talk to the person in your family who you have chosen every day.

4. There are lots of different words that you can use that mean the same as 'hello' or 'goodbye' – ask the adult or friend that you are working with to think of some of these with you.

5. Make sure that you understand the need for family rules.

Chapter

FRIENDSHIPS AND RELATIONSHIPS

People who have an ASD often find it hard to make friends.

People with an ASD also find it hard to understand what other people are thinking and feeling. Lots of people with an ASD find that they feel lonely because making, understanding and keeping friends is hard. This part of the book will help you to learn more about friends and other types of relationships like boyfriends and girlfriends. This part of the book should also help you learn about what it means to have friendships or relationships with someone.

Why is it a good idea to make friends?

If you make friends you can:

- spend time with somebody who likes the same things as you
- play games that need two people, e.g. chess or tennis
- learn more about things that interest you both
- work together and help each other solve problems
- practise and improve your social skills.

What is friendship?

People have different sorts of friends. The word used to describe having friends is 'friendships'.

There are different levels of friendship that you can have. These levels of friendships depend upon lots of things. Levels of friendships start with a basic or simple friend. A basic or simple friend is a person that you know and like.

Good friends or best friends (a higher level of friendship) have more to them than just somebody that you know and like. If you say that somebody is a good friend then you need to understand what a good friend is. On the next page you will learn more about what a good friend is.

It is important to understand that friendships take time to develop: more than just a few weeks. It is also important to understand that friendships mean that two people do the same sorts of things for each other, like saying hello to each other or helping each other. You cannot buy or own a friend in the same way as you can an object.

You might find that your friends change from time to time. Sometimes this happens because you move on to a different school or change jobs. You might also find that you and your friends begin to be interested in different things so you have less to talk about. When your life changes and you grow up you may have different friends.

It is okay to have more than one friend. It is okay for your friend to have other friends as well. You might have lots of friends or you might have one or two special friends. The number of friends that you have will change as you get older and you might have more friends as you grow up or you might have fewer friends. It is okay for this to happen and it happens to everybody in the world.

There are lots of different types of friendships. The list below is not complete but it is just to give you some ideas:

Friends do these things

- Know each other's name.

- See each other at school or at work.

- Say hello to each other when you see each other.

70

- Talk to each other when you see each other.

- Listen to what each other says.

- Like each other.

- Try not to hurt each other.

- Sometimes help each other at school or at work.

- Sometimes play together or talk together.

- Don't ask you to do things that are wrong.

- Don't ask you to do things that may get you into trouble.

- Don't ask you to do things that are dangerous.

Good friends do these things

All of the things a friend does, plus some others:

- Know the names of some people in each other's family.

- Have some similar interests.

- Often play or talk together at school or work.

- Sometimes share toys or equipment.

- Sometimes see each other in the evenings or at weekends.

- Help each other.

- Look after each other when one of the friends is upset.

- Know each other's likes and dislikes.

- Make each other laugh.

Best friends do these things

All of the things a good friend does, plus some others:

- Trust each other (that means telling the truth and trying hard to do what they say they will do).

- Have a lot of contact (that means seeing each other, talking on the telephone for a few minutes, writing letters, sending text messages or emails to each other).

- Always help each other when they can.

- Try hard not to say unkind things to each other.

- Give each other advice – that means telling each other what could be done differently to make a situation better.

- Keep each other's secrets.

How to make friends

- Ask someone their name.

- Tell them your name.

- Ask them what they like to do or what they are interested in.

- Tell them your interests.

- Remember to ask questions about the other person's interests and talk about their interests, not just your own interests.

- Try to find out if you have something in common (that means something that you both like).

How to build up a friendship

If you have just met or made a friend then the next thing to do is to build up your friendship so that you get to know your friend better. Here are some ideas about how you can build up a friendship.

- Try to see each other at least once a week.

- Remember to smile and say hello when you see your friend to show them that you like them.

- Plan to do things together like watch a DVD or play a video game.

- Try to find more things in common (that means things that you both like doing).

- Ask each other questions to find out more about what each of you like or think about something.

- Remember to be kind to each other all of the time.

- Say sorry to each other if you have said or done something to upset each other.

- Talk to people in your family and find out if your friend can visit your house.

- Talk to each other whenever you see each other about what you have been doing.

- Each time you meet, plan the next time that you will see each other.

Activity 15: Friend checklist

Have you made a new friend?

Put a tick ☑ in the box if you agree or a cross ☒ in the box if you don't.

If you have met someone who might be a friend, check that you **both**:

☐   know each other's name

☐   see each other regularly (e.g. at school, work or at a club)

☐   say hello to each other when you meet

☐   talk to each other

☐   have similar (that means the same or nearly the same) interests

☐   like doing similar things

☐   say positive (that means good or helpful) things to each other

☐   don't annoy or irritate each other

☐   help each other

☐   share things with each other

☐   don't ask each other to do things that are wrong or dangerous.

If you have ticked all of the boxes then you have made a new friend – if not, don't worry. You can work towards these things whenever you meet someone who you think might become your friend.

What is a boyfriend or girlfriend?

The words 'boyfriend' and 'girlfriend' usually have a special meaning. Boyfriends and girlfriends are like best friends but you will do other things with a boyfriend or girlfriend that you would not do with a friend. Having a boyfriend or girlfriend is called 'having a relationship'. Boyfriends or girlfriends start like any other friendship but they will also include other things. If you have a boyfriend or girlfriend sometimes people will say that you are 'going out' with them. If you say or hear the phrase that you are 'going out with someone' this usually means that you have a boyfriend or girlfriend.

The other things that you do with a boyfriend or girlfriend are physical things (like holding hands or kissing). The physical things that you do with a boyfriend or girlfriend make having a boyfriend or girlfriend different to having friends.

Occasionally people may use the word 'boyfriend' to mean a boy that is also a friend. Occasionally people may use the word 'girlfriend' to mean a girl that is also a friend.

Meeting the right boyfriend or girlfriend

Because all boyfriends and girlfriends usually start as friends, you can follow the list for friends. Boyfriends and girlfriends also have something extra that you need to think about. After some time you will have some physical contact. Physical contact with a boyfriend or girlfriend usually starts during teenage years. It is important to remember that having a boyfriend or a girlfriend means having a two-way relationship – you both have to like each other and be interested in what each other is doing or saying.

If a friend is going to be a boyfriend or girlfriend you need to be attracted to each other. Being attracted to each other means that you like the way the other person looks, and you like the way that they do things (for example, the way they laugh or the clothes that they wear) and more than your other friends.

People are usually supposed to have just one boyfriend or girlfriend at a time and, in the future, if you decide to get married or have a partnership with someone then only having one boyfriend, girlfriend, wife or husband will become very important.

You should think about whether or not it is a good idea to tell your boyfriend or girlfriend that you have an ASD. If you spend a lot of time with your boyfriend or girlfriend then it might be a good idea to talk to them about your ASD. If you have just met, or started to go out with, your boyfriend or girlfriend you might not want to tell them that you have an ASD until you get to know them well.

Activity 16: Boyfriend or girlfriend checklist

If you have met someone who you think might become a boyfriend or girlfriend then do this checklist again, plus these extra points.

Put a tick ☑ in the box if you agree or a cross ☒ in the box if you don't.

For a boyfriend or girlfriend do you *both*:

☐   like the way you both behave

☐   like the way you both look

☐   like to have some physical contact with each other

☐   not want to have physical contact with someone else

☐   enjoy each other's company.

If you have ticked all of the boxes above then you might have found a boyfriend or girlfriend. If not, then you could have made a new friend.

What to do next

1. Read through the points on the checklist in Activity 15 (and then the points on the checklist in Activity 16 if you have filled this in) to see if you need to find out any more information about your friends.

2. If you do need more information, then talk to an adult or someone older in your family and ask them if they can help you to find out this information.

3. If you have all of the information you need then talk to an adult or someone in your family about either:

    o   finding a new friend

        or

    o   finding a boyfriend or girlfriend

        or

    o   making a basic friend a good friend or a good friend a best friend.

4. Make a list of three things that you could do to improve your friendships like inviting a friend to your house for tea, but make sure that this is okay with the rest of your family first.

5. Try to do at least one of these things in the next two weeks.

6. If you need to know more about your friend's friends, then you could draw a friendship map, like the example opposite, to show friendships.

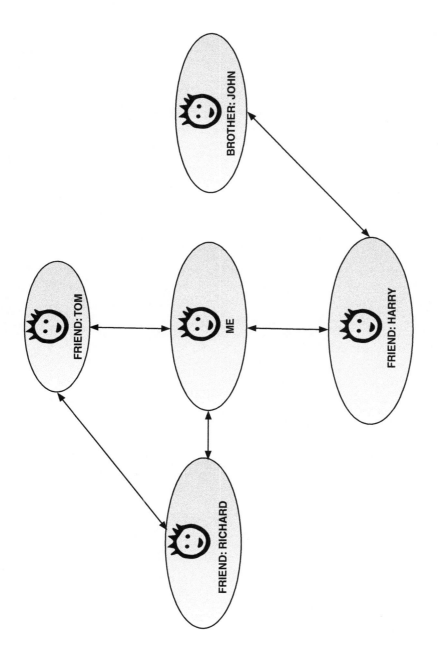

Example of a friendship map: this shows the connections between different friends

Chapter **6**

STRENGTHS
AND INTERESTS

What are strengths and interests?

Everybody has strengths and interests.

- A strength is something that you are good at.

- An interest is something that you enjoy doing or something that you want to learn more about.

It is important to understand your own strengths and interests. You can use your strengths and interests to make your life easier – for example, if you are good at using a computer then you could type letters instead of writing them or use the internet to help you with your homework or tasks that you have to do at work. You can also develop your strengths and interests to find the right job for you. The best job to have is a job that you can do well and that you are interested in.

If you are good at your work and interested in your work then you will not find your job hard or boring. Unfortunately, a lot of people who do not have an ASD say that their jobs are hard or boring. If you have an ASD you will probably have different strengths and interests to other people – this could mean that you are able to find a job that other people don't find interesting.

Why is it important to recognise your strengths and interests?

Here is a list of five reasons why you should work out what your main strengths and interests are, and then develop or improve them.

1. You will be able to enjoy school or work more.

2. Tasks at work or school will be easier for you – this means that they will not make you feel worried about getting jobs done.

3. You will be able to think about and try to plan your future around what you like doing – a lot of people who do not have an ASD have difficulty knowing what course they want to take or what jobs they want to do.

4. You will be able to meet people with the same strengths and interests – these people will probably be easier for you to talk to.

5. If you develop your strengths and interests you will always have something to do that you enjoy and you will not feel bored.

6. Having a strength or an interest can also help you to feel more confident about yourself because you know that there are things that you are good at.

How are your strengths and interests different to those of people without an ASD?

People with an ASD may have different strengths and interests to people who do not have an ASD. People who don't have an ASD may be good at and may like to:

- work with people
- just be with people and chat about unimportant matters
- not always follow rules
- not always work through things in a systematic way but sometimes do things in no order whatsoever

- vary the way they do things from day to day

- avoid routines that sometimes seem boring

- try new things

- have surprises and not have any warnings or preparations for things, e.g. surprise parties.

People with an ASD are quite different. People with an ASD may be good at, or like doing, these types of things:

- designing or following systems, e.g. computers

- technical subjects, e.g. mechanics

- areas that involve precision ('precision' means being absolutely correct about each and every detail), e.g. engineering

- collections, e.g. Lego or stamp collections

- following strict rules and guidelines, e.g. when making or manufacturing things

- keeping to planned routines and schedules, and doing things in the same order.

Why might your strengths and interests cause difficulties?

This is mainly because of a lack of understanding between people who don't have an ASD and people who have an ASD. People with an ASD find it hard to realise that trying new things, doing things differently and having surprises can be a lot of fun for neurotypical people. (Neurotypical is a word used to describe people who do not have autism.) People who don't have an ASD have difficulty understanding why routines, systems and rules are so important and pleasing for people with an ASD.

You will probably realise that, when it comes to strengths and interests, people with an ASD and people who don't have an ASD sometimes have opposite strengths and interests. In fact, what makes you feel safe and happy may well make people who don't have an ASD feel bored and unhappy. The things that make people who don't have an ASD feel happy and safe might make you feel worried or scared. People with an ASD and people who don't have an ASD may not understand each other's strengths and interests and this can lead to problems. If you enjoy doing something or really need to do something then it might be hard for neurotypical people to realise that your needs are different to theirs.

People with an ASD may feel that people who don't have an ASD are disorganised or are not keeping routines just to be annoying. People who don't have an ASD may feel that people with an ASD are just trying to ruin their fun or take over a situation – this is called being too bossy or 'domineering'.

The ability to focus on things is a strength that most people with an ASD have. This strength may mean that people with ASD often find it hard to stop thinking about or talking about their interests.

It is important to understand that your strengths and interests may change as you get older. People in your family might remember what you used to like when you were younger – you could ask them to tell you what things you were good at when you were small and what things you used to like doing.

Activity 17: Learning about strengths and interests

I used to be good at . . . .

. . . .

I used to like . . . .

. . . .

Make a list of five things that you are good at. Ask other people in your family or adults and pupils at school what they think that you are good at – you will probably have more strengths than you think!

I am good at:

1. . . . .

. . . .

2. . . . .

. . . .

3. . . . .

. . . .

4. . . . .

. . . .

5. . . . .

. . . .

Now make a list of the things that you are interested in:

I am interested in:

1. ....

   ....

2. ....

   ....

3. ....

   ....

4. ....

   ....

5. ....

   ....

Activity 18: Developing your strengths and interests

Look at the lists that you made of your strengths and your interests. With an adult, try to join a strength with an interest. For example, if you are good at drawing designs and you are interested in computers, then you could try computer aided design (CAD). When you have done this, fill in the table below.

Strength	Interest	I could try...
Drawing designs	Computers	CAD

Activity 19: Managing your strengths and interests

You may have some very particular interests that you think about or talk about for long periods of time. It can cause a problem if you find it hard to stop thinking about these interests and find it hard to concentrate on other things. It is a good idea to try to manage your interests if this happens.

'Managing your interests' means that you will have a set time or place to think about or keep your interests. This will be very helpful for other people who get annoyed with you if they think that your interests take up too much time or space. It will also be helpful for you because you will find that you have less of a problem with other people getting annoyed with you.

Have a look at the lists that you made of your strengths and your interests. Usually strengths or interests fit into these two groups:

- collections – objects or other things that you keep, e.g. Lego, cards or magazines
- activities – things that you like to do, e.g. using the internet, remembering parts of TV shows, playing video games or writing lists.

Here are some ideas for you to talk about with a friend or an adult in your family:

Collections

It is important to keep collections tidy and organised in a way that doesn't take up too much space. If you have a large collection, or a lot of something, it may be a good idea to catalogue your collection. Cataloguing means having a list of what you have and where you keep it. This will help you to know that your collection is safe and that you can find things in your collection whenever you need to.

Another important thing about collections is to have the right storage system. This means a suitable book, box or shelf to keep your collection in. The adult who you are working with will have some ideas about how to keep your collections safe and tidy, and not taking up too much space in your house.

Make a list of any collections that you have and think of a way in which these collections are stored. If you do not have any collections then just write 'N/A' in the chart – this stands for 'not applicable' and means that you do not have anything to write down.

If you have a friend who likes to collect the same things as you then you might want to show them your collection. If you do decide to show other people your collection then they might want to touch some items in your collection. You may find it very difficult if other people touch or move your collections. If other people touch or move your collections then you may want to learn about how you might overcome this feeling. If you feel like this then it would be a good idea to explain this to other people so that they understand how you feel about your collections. Talk to the adult or friend who is working through this book with you about this.

Some people might like to trade things in their collections (swap or exchange one thing for another). Lots of people trade or swap their cards if they have more than one of the same card. You might want to ask an adult or friend if a trade is fair (where you swap or exchange things that are the same price or are as important as each other) or not, and then decide if you want to trade anything in your collection.

Activity 20: Managing collections

Things I collect	I could keep them in…
Stamps	A book

Activities

It is important to fit your special activities and hobbies in with other things that you need to do. You might not realise how much time you spend on these things and you might find it hard to stop. Other people will get annoyed with you if they think that you have spent too much time on an activity, or if you have difficulty stopping an activity when you need to do something else.

It is important to decide, with a friend or an adult, when you can do your activity and how long for. The friend or adult that you are working with will understand that your activities are important and special to you. The friend or adult will let you have a time and a place for your activity so you don't get into trouble. They will also help you to decide if you need another person to help you and to agree on a suitable length of time to spend on your activity.

Activity 21: Managing activities

Activity	When I can do this	Who with	How long for
Games console	Every day at 6.30pm	Take turns with my brother	3 turns of 5 minutes each, a total time of 30 minutes for both of us

What to do next

1. Make sure that you understand how your strengths and your interests can help you, but also that they have to be fitted in with everyday life.

2. Look through the charts that you have filled in and ask any questions that you need to.

3. If you have a collection that needs cataloguing then make a list of everything that you have. Ask an adult for help if you need to.

4. If you have a collection that needs storing then talk to an adult about when, where and how to find, make or buy storage equipment.

5. Remember to go through these charts and lists again if your interests change.

Chapter **7**

SCHOOL

Why do people have to go to school?

The law in most countries makes education for children and young people compulsory. This means that every child or young person must go to school until they are a certain age. Going to school is important because:

- you will learn how to do important things like reading and writing

- you will be able to study different subjects and find out which subjects you like best

- you will meet other people

- you will find out things that will help you as you grow older, e.g. how to make things

- you will learn skills that are important for work.

Some secondary schools will arrange for pupils to do some work experience. Work experience is spending some time with a company or organisation that you are interested in to learn more about what it is like to have a job there. An example might be working in a supermarket, hospital or a bank. Work experience also gives you the opportunity to see what it is like to do a type of job like working with computers or fixing cars.

When young people become adults it is usually expected that they will have a job and go to work at some time in their adult lives, and going to school prepares you for this. Having a job will help you to become more independent. You will have some money to spend on the things that you want. You may also meet new friends, learn new skills and develop new interests.

If you wanted to find out more about what it is like to have a job and work in different organisations you could find out about voluntary work. Voluntary work means that you have a job to go to but you don't actually get paid for it. Lots of charities (organisations that help people) use volunteers to do most of their work. Ask the adult who is helping you to complete this book about what sort of volutary work might be available near to where you live.

Another way to find out what it is like to go to work is to have a job at weekends. You can still go to school during the week but you can also work on a Saturday or Sunday. Lots of shops and supermarkets have weekend jobs. Some of your friends might have a weekend job.

Why school may sometimes be a challenge for you if you have an ASD

There are three main reasons why school may be a challenge for you:

1. *Understanding* – you will be expected to know or learn things that you could find hard.

2. *Social demands* – there will be other people who you will have to talk to or work with.

3. *Sensory sensitivity* – you may have sensory difficulties, e.g. with noise or smells.

Talk to the adult who is helping you with this workbook about:

1. whether you need to tell someone that you have an ASD

2. who you should talk to at school

3. when to talk to them

4. what to say to them.

Activity 22: Difficulties at school

Most people, whether they have an ASD or not, have some problems at some point at school. Below is a checklist that lists some of the problems that people with an ASD may face at school. It is important that you know about your own problems with school because then you will be able to solve these problems. The following checklists will help you to think about what problems you have with school and then you can begin to solve these problems.

Put a tick ☑ in the box if you agree or a cross ☒ in the box if you don't.

Difficulties with understanding

☐ I am not always sure what some words mean.

☐ It takes me a long time to think about information.

☐ I need help to organise my work.

☐ I lose things.

☐ I find it hard to explain things.

☐ I don't like tests or answering questions.

☐ I get upset if I don't think that I can finish my work in time.

☐ I don't like writing a lot of words.

☐ I don't like making mistakes.

☐ I like to have a visual timetable so that I know what to expect.

☐ I don't understand why I have to do homework when I have finished school for the day.

Social demands

☐ I don't like places where there are a lot of people.

☐ I get confused about what people really mean.

☐ It is hard for me to talk to people that I don't know.

☐ I don't understand people's jokes.

☐ I prefer to work on my own.

☐ Working in a group or a team is hard for me.

☐ I prefer work times to break times.

☐ I don't like it if people get too close to me.

☐ Other people are interested in different things to me.

☐ I get frustrated if I have to wait for other people.

☐ I find it hard to know if other people are being unkind or just gently teasing me.

☐ Other people don't understand my needs.

Sensory issues

☐ Sometimes school is too noisy.

☐ I don't like the smell of some parts of my school.

☐ I prefer to eat on my own.

☐ The uniform is uncomfortable.

☐ I don't like the smell or taste of the food.

☐ The lights or the computer hurts my eyes.

☐ There are some sounds that are uncomfortable for me.

☐ I really don't like the way some equipment feels.

☐ Some of the displays are distracting.

☐ I prefer to bring my own food or drink to school.

Thinking about school

It is important that you know that going to school or college has a real purpose. Having a purpose means that you will get something from doing something. At school you might meet people that you like and you can get some qualifications. Qualifications are exams or courses that will mean you are able to prove to employers or universities that you can complete a course or do a certain job. Qualifications are also important for real-life skills like understanding money or learning how to cook.

Remember that everybody finds some part of school hard – ask the adult or friend that you are working with what they found hard about school.

Activity 23: Thinking about school

Think about three things that you find most difficult about school. You can work out ideas to help yourself with these difficulties in the next chapter.

The three things that I find most difficult about school are:

1. ....

....

2. ....

....

3. ....

....

Now think about three things that you enjoy about school. In the next chapter you can use the things that you enjoy about school to help you to find solutions to your difficulties.

The three things that I like about school are:

1. ....

....

2. ....

....

3. ....

....

What you can do to improve what school is like for you

If there are things about your school that you find hard then you could try the ten ideas listed below to make these things easier for you. These ten ideas will be useful for everything that you have to do at school.

1. Always find out exactly what you have to do.

2. Ask for help if you need it – remember that the adults in charge at your school are there to help you. It is a good idea to find out one or two people who you can talk to about any problems that you might have with school.

3. Try to think about exactly what the problem is and explain the problem to people – you will need to actually tell other people what is wrong.

4. Make a list using words or pictures for important things that you have to remember.

5. Make a list using words or pictures for important things that you have to do each day and put a tick next to things that you have finished.

6. Keep a diary and note down deadlines – deadlines are when work must be completed or handed in to somebody.

7. If you make a mistake then stop, think and try again.

8. Find out and learn the rules of your school.

9. Try to make some friends so that you can help each other.

10. Find out where things are kept so that you can use what you need for your work – remember to put these things back.

How you can plan your career

A 'career' is the type of job that you do. The best careers use your strengths and your interests. Careers are based in different 'fields' – this does not mean a piece of land with grass: it means something completely different. When it comes to careers, fields are subjects or a theme of work, for example, the field of education includes teachers, university lecturers and administrators; the field of medicine includes nurses, doctors and surgeons.

Finding the field that you are interested in and have the right talents to work in is a good way to start planning what you would like to do.

It is important to remember that you might not be able to do the job that you want to straight away. Developing a career involves lots of hard work and you may have to study for qualifications that could take several years. Ask the adult or friend who is working through this book with you about what your chosen career actually involves because it is very important to be realistic about what you want to do.

Activity 24: Six steps to plan your career

There are six steps to choosing a career. When you are ready to think about your career, you can work through this section with a friend or adult. If you need to, you can work through each step one at a time because there is a lot of information to record. Don't worry if you have to complete this activity over a few days.

Look at the table that you made about your strengths and interests on page 87.

Step 1: Your interests

Write your five favourite interests in order – start with the thing that you like best.

1. ....

....

2. ....

....

3. ....

....

4. ....

....

5. ....

....

Write your five best strengths in order – start with the thing that you are best at.

1. . . . .

. . . .

2. . . . .

. . . .

3. . . . .

. . . .

4. . . . .

. . . .

5. . . . .

. . . .

Step 2: Your skills

Next you need to think about what your skills are. Skills are like strengths but they are more exact. Skills are things that you have learned to do. Skills usually need practice and time to develop. If one of your strengths is working carefully then a skill that you might have learned is neat handwriting.

Below is a list of skills. You might need to add more to the list.

Put a tick ☑ in the box if you agree or a cross ☒ in the box if you don't.

My skills are

☐ attending to details

☐ computer skills

☐ counting accurately

☐ creating new ideas

☐ handwriting

☐ organisation

☐ problem solving

☐ reading

☐ time management

☐ working methodically.

Write in here other strengths that are not on the list above:

1. ....

   ....

2. ....

   ....

3. ....

   ....

Step 3: Choosing a career field

Below is a list of the main career fields.

Put a tick ☑ in the box if you are interested in this field or a cross ☒ in the box if you aren't.

If you can't find the career field that fits in with your interests then ask a friend or adult to help you to find out one that does.

☐ Agriculture (farming)

☐ Animals (looking after animals – for example, in a zoo or dog-walking)

☐ Banking (dealing with people's money)

☐ Business (making money)

☐ Care sector (looking after people)

☐ Cleaning (in people's homes or an organisation)

☐ Design (making plans for things)

☐ Drama (acting or writing scripts for actors)

☐ Education (teaching)

☐ Engineering (making machines or fixing things)

☐ Leisure (working in hotels or sports centres)

☐ Information and Communication Technology (Computers)

☐ Law (working with the police or for a court)

☐ Manufacturing (making things with machines)

☐ Medicine (finding cures for illnesses)

☐ Nursing (helping people who are sick)

☐   Retail (shop work)

☐   Science (investigating how the world works)

Other career fields that I am interested in that are not on the list:

1. ....

    ....

2. ....

    ....

3. ....

    ....

4. ....

    ....

5. ....

    ....

Step 4: Choosing a career

Now that you have had a chance to think about your interests, strengths and skills you can begin to think about your career. Don't worry if you can't decide on a career straight away. It is always useful to think about the career field that you would like to work in, or to think about the different kinds of jobs that you may want to do. Thinking about and planning your career is useful even if you don't know exactly what job you would like.

Step 5: Qualifications

Now that you have thought about the types of jobs you *could* do you can begin to find out about the qualifications that you need. Eventually you will need to know how, where and when you can get these qualifications.

Finding a career

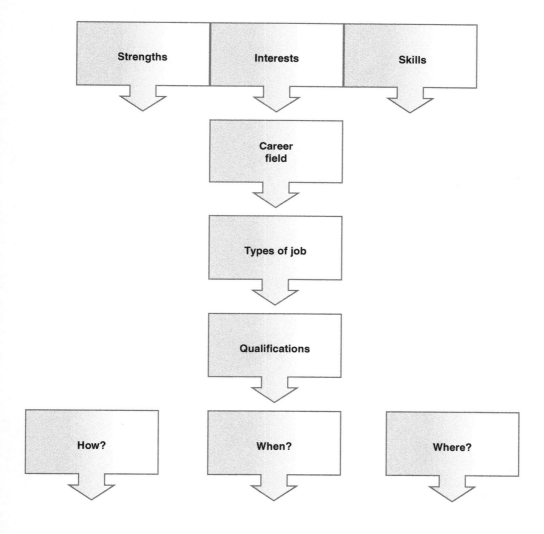

The jobs that I would like to do are:

....

....

....

....

....

....

....

....

....

....

Job applications

Before you start a job or work experience you might have to do two things:

1. Fill out an application form.

2. Have an interview.

Application forms

These are forms that have spaces in them for you to write or type your personal details. Personal details include your name, address and your date of birth. You will probably also have to write or type any qualifications that you have (for example, a GCSE). Most application forms also ask if you have already had any other jobs or work experience. There will also be a space for you to write or type a few sentences about why you would like the job and what skills you have that mean that you can do the job.

Don't worry about filling in application forms. The adult who is helping you with this workbook will also be able to help you fill in an application form.

Interviews

An interview for a job is when you talk to a person or some people who already work an organisation. They will ask you questions about why you would like the job that you are applying for and how your own skills, or what you are learning at school, will help you to do the job. The people asking you questions about the job will probably ask you to give some more information about what you have written on the application form.

Most people feel a little bit nervous about job interviews but the best way to help you learn what to do at an interview is to practise. The adult who is helping you with this book could help you to practise some interviews. Most secondary schools will also be able to help you with interviews.

If you do find a weekend or voluntary job or have some work experience at your school then you should think about whether or not to tell people that you have an ASD. You should talk to the person helping you to fill in the section about telling other people that you have a diagnosis of autism.

What to do next

1. Make sure that you have completed the three checklists about school or work (*Difficulties with understanding, Social demands* and *Sensory issues*).

2. Talk to the adult or friend who you are working with about what they like or dislike about school or work.

3. If you feel ready, then work through the section about choosing a career.

4. If you need to find out about qualifications then you can ask a friend or adult to help. There is a lot of information about careers and qualifications on the internet.

5. Make a list of the jobs that you think that you would like to do.

Chapter **8**

GETTING HELP

What is self-help?

Getting help means being able to develop ways to overcome difficulties. Self-help includes thinking about solving your own problems. Self-help does not mean that you have to sort out all of your difficulties on your own, but it does mean that you can make decisions about who to talk to and how you use the advice that you have been given by other people.

Why do you need to develop ways to help yourself?

Everybody has problems and difficulties at some time in their lives. When you are at school or starting a new job people will always think that you might need some help even if you don't ask for it – for example, with writing or knowing what to do next. As you grow older you might find that people think that you are okay unless you tell them that something is wrong.

What might you need help with?

If you have an ASD you might need help with the following.

Getting organised

Many people with an ASD find it hard to organise themselves. Usually this means that they have problems with remembering all the things that have to be done and knowing what order to do things in. However, once people with an ASD have learned a routine, or way of doing things, then they are usually very good at following routines. The important thing about getting organised is to work with somebody who can help you remember each step that is needed to complete an activity. You can use self-help to get organised by thinking through exactly what you have to do, then listing the steps that you need to take to achieve this.

Making friends

Most people with an ASD want to make friends and enjoy spending time with these friends. In this workbook you have already thought through some ideas about how to make friends. You can also use the self-help plan at the end of this chapter to make a detailed plan about how to make friends with people you know or would like to meet.

Social skills

Having an ASD will mean that you are likely to need help with various social skills from time to time. There are many different social skills that people need to have and you have probably learned a lot of them already but there may be some social skills that you need to practise. You can work through the self-help plan at the end of this chapter to identify which social skills you need to develop, and then plan to improve these social skills.

Resolving disagreements

Everybody has a dispute or disagreement with other people at some time in their lives. Most disputes are down to misunderstandings when two people see the same situation differently. The way to solve disputes is to try to understand what the other person thinks or to try to see their views and why they hold these views. The self-help plan at the end of this chapter can be used to provide a method for understanding other people's views, and then you can work out a way to sort out your difficulties.

Sensory issues

Some sensory problems will be easy to solve – for example, if you don't like the feel of a certain fabric then you could wear clothes that are made from a different fabric. Other sensory problems might be more difficult. The more difficult sensory problems that you might face are things that occur in your environment that will be hard to remove, like the sound of central heating or the sight of certain food that other people in your family really like to eat. For the more difficult sensory problems you can use the self-help plan to find a way to cope with the sensory problem or problems that you are having.

Self-help plan

This is a plan to help you solve really big problems that you have, like problems that stop you from sleeping or problems that are making you really anxious. It is important that you talk to a parent or an adult about your problem and about filling in the self-help plan.

The way to solve problems is to work through steps so that you can understand more about your problem and then think of different ways to solve it. To help you to think through your problem there are questions for you that will help you to think about each step. Each of the questions that you need to answer is explained first of all and, at the end of this chapter, there is a blank self-help plan that you can use to fill in your own answers.

Step 1: Explain the problem

Remember that there are some things that you will *have* to do even if you find them difficult – for example, going to school or work. It is important to remember that there will always be a way to make difficult things easier, even if you cannot completely remove the problem. If there are things that you find hard then you can be sure that some other people will also find these things hard.

It is also important to consider if the problem is actually yours to solve – sometimes problems that you think are yours to solve are really the responsibility of other people – for example, your parents or people who work for governments.

To answer the first question you need to make a note of exactly what the problem is. You may also need to explain the problem to other people who might not know that you have a problem. Sometimes, once you have explained your problem to someone else, they will be able to solve it straight away. If the problem cannot be solved straight away then you can go to Step 2.

Step 2: Getting help

Getting help for yourself can mean asking somebody to help you with a problem. Getting help for yourself can also mean finding information that will help you work through your problem. You can help yourself in lots of different ways – here are some ideas.

BOOKS

There are many different types of books designed to help people work through the problems that they have. These books include subjects like getting the right job, study skills, managing money or dealing with feeling anxious or depressed. The advantage of using books is that you can always have them nearby when you need to look at. You will find the books listed in the 'Recommended reading' in Chapter 9 helpful.

USING THE INTERNET

The internet can be used to search for information or to join forums.

'Forums' are websites where people contact each other, and you may find a forum for other people with an ASD so that you can discuss any issues about ASDs. Forums can also be used to talk about things that interest you and there are all kinds of different forums for a wide variety of subjects.

Always use the internet carefully. There is so much information and so many different people using the internet that it is important to be careful about how reliable or correct the information is. It is a good idea to search for information or forums on the internet with an adult present, and to start your search by using the recommended websites that are listed in Chapter 9 of this workbook.

TALKING TO FRIENDS OR RELATIVES

You will probably find that the people in your family know you very well and so they will be able to give you advice or help that is appropriate and reliable. If you have some friends who you trust well then they will also be helpful. Your friends and family will probably have information about you, your school or your work so they will think about this information when they help you to deal with any problems that you might have.

GROUPS

Joining a group is a good idea if you want to meet people who have similar interests to you. Joining a group is also a good way to get help and advice for problems. Groups may be designed around interests (for example, a model train collectors' club) or they may be support groups designed to help people (for example, a support group to help young people find work. Groups are sometimes associated with having a faith or belonging to a religion.

JOINING A GROUP

If you want to join a group you will have to find out the following information:

1. *The name of the group that you want to join* – ask the adult who is helping you with this book to help you: you might find this information on the internet or at a library

2. *When the group meets* – the group might only meet when you are at school.

3. *Where the group meets* – remember that you will have to find a way to travel to and from the group.

4. *If there are any age limits* – some groups might just be for children or some groups might be just for adults.

5. *What you have to do to join* – you might have to fill in a form or pay some money to the person who organises the group.

COUNSELLING AT SCHOOL

Most schools have staff whose job it is to deal with personal problems. Schools may also run a counselling service. If you are thinking about counselling then make sure that you talk to a parent or an adult about this first. You will also need to make sure that the counsellor who you talk to understands about ASDs.

Counselling means talking to someone about difficult situations but this usually means talking to somebody that you don't know but who is trained to listen and help. Sometimes it is easier to talk to somebody that you don't know because the advice that they give you will be impartial advice. This means that the advice is not affected by the way somebody who knew you well might feel about a situation. Impartial advice is also non-judgemental. This means that you will be given help or ideas about what to do without somebody thinking that you have made bad mistakes and telling you that you have been wrong or foolish.

Step 3: Find solutions to your problem

Now that you have explained your problem and thought about the sort of help that is available, you can think about finding solutions to solve your problem. In Step 3 you will need to think of different things that might help you.

Try to think of between three to five different ways that you could solve your problem. Think about the advantages (the good or positive things) and disadvantages (the bad or negative things) for each solution. There is an example of this below. Remember that a disadvantage is not always a reason for not doing something but it is just something to think about to help you to decide what to do.

118

The problem: Maths homework is too difficult for me

	Solution 1	Solution 2	Solution 3	Solution 4	Solution 5
	Spend more time at home and use a maths book to help me to understand	Forget about being better at maths and focus on other subjects	Don't do maths homework	Ask a teacher or teaching assistant to help me	Join a maths homework club
Advantages					
	I will learn more about maths	I will have something more interesting to think about	Problem seems to go away	A teacher or teaching assistant will be able to explain things in a way that I can understand	I will get help with the work that I am doing at school
Disadvantages					
	I already have too much homework to do	My maths might not get easier or improve. I might not get the qualifications that I need for a job	Not possible. I will get detentions and maybe even more maths homework as a punishment	A teacher or teaching assistant might not be able to help straight away – I may have to wait	I might have to travel home from school alone

Step 4: Set clear aims and objectives

Now that you have thought about different ways that you could solve your problem you will need to decide on the solution that you think is the right one for you. Once you have done this then you will need to set yourself a clear aim. An aim means one idea that you will try to do. For example:

- Aim: Join a maths homework club to get help with maths homework.

OBJECTIVES

When you have an aim you can set objectives. Objectives are the different stages that you need to go through to reach your aim. It is a good idea to set at least one objective to do within a certain time. If you have completed an objective then you can cross it off the list and write a note if you need to. Below are some examples:

~~Find out when maths homework club is.~~ Wednesday 3.30 pm.

Find out how to join maths homework club.

Ask Mum or Dad to help me get home after school.

Find out where maths homework club takes place.

Go to maths homework club for five weeks.

Step 5: Check to see if the plan is working

There are two ways that you can review your plan. The first way is to check to see if you have completed all of your objectives. The second way is to ask yourself, 'Has my plan solved the problem, or made it easier for me to deal with?'

For the example above you could look at your list of objectives and see if they are all crossed off the list. Then you would ask yourself, 'Is maths home-work easier for me to do now?'

Now look at the diagram on page 122, which shows you how the self-help plan works as a whole.

If you have a problem but feel that the self-help plan is too much to work through or that the problem is just a small problem then then try a simpler approach:

- Explain – tell someone about the problem.

- Ask – ask for help if you need to.

- Try – try to follow the advice that you have been given.

Some things to think about

1. Remember that everybody has problems at some time in their life!

2. Ask a friend or adult who you are working with if there is anything that you don't understand about self-help

3. If you have a problem that is worrying you then work through the blank self-help plan in Activity 25.

4. Remember, if you have a problem but feel that the self-help plan is too much to work through then try the simpler approach:

    o Explain – tell someone about the problem.

    o Ask – ask for help if you need to.

    o Try – try to follow the advice that you have been given.

5. You could think about making a list of the problems that you have had and how you managed to solve them. This will remind you that problems can be made easier and it might also help you solve other problems.

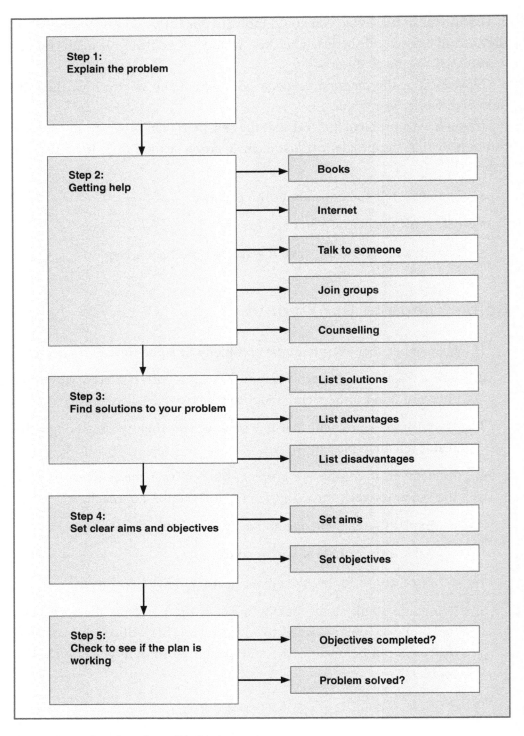

Step 1:
Explain the problem

Step 2:
Getting help

Books

Internet

Talk to someone

Join groups

Counselling

Step 3:
Find solutions to your problem

List solutions

List advantages

List disadvantages

Step 4:
Set clear aims and objectives

Set aims

Set objectives

Step 5:
Check to see if the plan is working

Objectives completed?

Problem solved?

A diagram to show how the self-help plan works

Activity 25: Self-help plan

Step 1: Explain the problem

My problem is . . . .

. . . .

. . . .

. . . .

. . . .

. . . .

Step 2: Getting help

Who can I ask?

I can ask these people:

1. . . . .

. . . .

2. . . . .

. . . .

3. . . . .

. . . .

4. . . . .

. . . .

5. . . . .

. . . .

What information might be helpful?

This information might be helpful:

1. . . . .

. . . .

2. . . . .

. . . .

3. . . . .

. . . .

4. . . . .

. . . .

5. . . . .

. . . .

Step 3: Find solutions to your problem

This activity should be completed if you already have a problem at work or school. If you don't have any problems now, you can use this activity in the future if you need to think about any problems you have then.

You can fill in this list below or you can use the chart below if you prefer. Talk to the friend or adult who you are working with to decide which layout is the best for you.

Solution 1 ....

Advantages

....

....

Disadvantages

....

....

Solution 2 ....

Advantages

....

....

Disadvantages

....

....

Solution 3 ....

Advantages

....

....

Disadvantages

....

....

Solution 4 ....

Advantages

....

....

Disadvantages

....

....

Solution 5 ....

Advantages

....

....

Disadvantages

....

....

If you do not want to complete the list on the previous pages you can use the chart below to find a solution to your problem.

The problem:				
Solution 1	Solution 2	Solution 3	Solution 4	Solution 5
Advantages				
Disadvantages				

Step 4: Set clear aims and objectives

Aim: . . . .

. . . .

Objectives:

1. . . . .

2. . . . .

3. . . . .

4. . . . .

5. . . . .

Step 5: Check to see if the plan is working

- Have I completed all of the objectives? Yes ☐ No ☐
- Has the plan solved the problem? Yes ☐ No ☐
- Has the plan made the problem easier? Yes ☐ No ☐
- Do I need to change my plan? Yes ☐ No ☐
- Do I need a new plan? Yes ☐ No ☐

You might need to change your plan and try a different solution. Don't worry if your problem isn't solved yet because by thinking about your problem you have already begun to make it easier. You might want to write a new plan if you have new ideas about how to solve your problem.

What to do next

1. Make sure that you understand the words used in this chapter – the Glossary in Chapter 10 explains some of the words used in this book.

2. Make a list of any problems that you are having but do not list more than ten.

3. With the friend or adult who you are working with, cross out any problems that are not your responsibility.

4. Choose the biggest problem that you have at the moment (just one problem) and work through the self-help plan with an adult.

5. Revise the self-help plan if you need to.

Chapter

FURTHER INFORMATION

Activity 26: Finding out about other people with an ASD

Look at the websites listed below, or find and then look through a book listed here for people who have an ASD. Find out about two other people who have an ASD.

Recommended reading for people with an ASD

What is Asperger Syndrome and How Will it Affect Me?
   Author: NAS Autism Helpline
   ISBN: 978 1 89928 014 8
   Published by The National Autistic Society, London.

Freaks, Geeks and Asperger Syndrome
   Author: Luke Jackson
   ISBN: 978 1 84310 098 0
   Published by Jessica Kingsley Publishers, London.

I Am Utterly Unique: Celebrating the Strengths of Children with Asperger Syndrome and High-functioning Autism
   Author: Elaine Marie Larson, illustrated by Vivian Strand
   ISBN: 978 1 93128 289 5
   Published by Autism Asperger Publishing Company, Overland Park, KS.

Different like Me: My Book of Autism Heroes
   Author: Jennifer Elder
   ISBN: 978 1 84310 815 3
   Published by Jessica Kingsley Publishers, London.

All Cats Have Asperger Syndrome
   Author: Kathy Hoopmann
   ISBN: 978 1 84310 481 0
   Published by Jessica Kingsley Publishers, London.

Aspects of Asperger's: Success in the Teens and Twenties
   Author: Maude Brown and Alex Miller
   ISBN: 978 1 90431 512 4
   Published by Lucky Duck Publishing, Bristol.

Recommended reading for parents and carers

Autism and the Family
   Author: Brenda Nally and E.V. Bliss
   Published by The National Autistic Society, London.

The Autistic Spectrum – A Parent's Guide
   Author: The National Autistic Society
   ISBN: 978 1 89928 008 7
   Published by The National Autistic Society, London.

Revealing the Hidden Social Code: Social Stories™ for People with Autism Spectrum Disorders
   Author: Marie Howley and Eileen Arnold
   ISBN: 978 1 84310 222 9
   Published by Jessica Kingsley Publishers, London.

Thinking in Pictures
   Author: Temple Grandin
   ISBN: 978 0 30773 958 2
   Published by Random House, New York.

Developing Talents
   Author: Temple Grandin and Kate Duffy
   ISBN: 978 1 93128 256 0
   Published by Autism Asperger Publishing Company, Overland Park, KS.

Websites for parents and carers

The National Autistic Society, UK

www.nas.org.uk

The National Autistic Society also has many local branches across the UK. You can find details of these branches on the NAS website.

Autism Speaks

www.autismspeaks.org

Based in the USA, this website contains a comprehensive collection of information and advice on advocacy.

Autism Connect

www.autismconnect.org.uk

This website contains lots of information about autism research and the latest news about autism.

Division TEACCH

www.teacch.com

Based at the University of North Carolina, USA, the TEACCH website contains references to research as well as practical guidance for parents and professionals.

Chapter **10**

GLOSSARY

Activity 27: Understanding words

Read the Glossary through to see if you understand all of the words in it. Put an asterisk (a small star like this: ✳) in pencil if you want to find out more about any of the words.

Activity – something that you do

Advantage – something that works well

Aim – something that you try to do

ASD – the capital letters stand for **a**utism **s**pectrum **d**isorder. ASDs mean having difficulties with being with other people (interacting), communication and imagination, or thinking about things

Asperger syndrome – the name given to the children whom Hans Asperger (a paediatrician, which means a doctor specialising in children's medicine) described in 1944 who had an ASD

Aunty – your mother or father's sister

Autism – the word first used by Leo Kanner (a paediatrician, which means a doctor specialising in children's medicine) in 1943 to describe people with an ASD

Boyfriend – a male who you are affectionate with

Career – the type of job that you do

Carer – someone who looks after you

Checklist – a list that you put a tick or cross next to

Civil partnerships – when two men or two women are officially declared a couple like being married

Co-habiting – two people who live together (this may be a man and a woman, two men or two women) but have not been officially married

Collection – a group of objects

Communication – this is how people let each other know their thoughts and feelings

Counselling – talking about difficult situations to somebody who you don't know but who is trained to listen to you and help you

Cousin – the son or daughter of your aunty or uncle

Daughter – a female child

Developing – making things better

Diagnosis – a test or assessment to find out what difficulties somebody has and to give a name to those difficulties

Disadvantage – something that does not work well

Divorce – when a marriage or civil partnership officially ends

Faith – the religious ideas that somebody believes in

Female – a girl or woman

Family – a group of people who are related to each other

Friend – a person who you know well

Girlfriend – a female who you are affectionate with

Grandfather – the father of your mother or father

Grandmother – the mother of your mother or father

Husband – the man a person is married to

Interaction – being in the same room or place as other people and responding to what they do

Interest – something you like doing or learning about

Job – something that you do and get paid for doing

Legal guardian – someone who has official powers to look after you (like your parents) but who is not your mother or father; a legal guardian may or may not be someone in your family

Male – a boy or man

Managing – organising things

Marriage – when a man and woman are legally declared a couple

Neurotypical – a word used to describe people who don't have autism

Objective – a way to reach an aim

Qualification – a certificate that shows you have passed a test or exam

Relative – someone who is in your family

Religion – organisations whose members believe in God

Rules – things that you have to try to do

Self-help – getting the help that you need, when you need it

Sensory sensitivity – being affected by noise, smell, light, touch or taste

Sibling – your sister, brother, stepsister or stepbrother

Son – a male child

Social skills – what you need to know or learn about understanding other people

Solution – an answer to a problem

Stepfather or stepmother – the husband or wife of your mother or father who is not your biological father or mother

Stepsister or stepbrother – brothers or sisters who do not have the same biological mother and father as you

Strength – something that you are good at

Tone – the stress put on words, for example, how loudly they are said or how high the voice sounds

Uncle – your mother or father's brother

Wife – the woman a person is married to

APPENDIX: PROGRESS CHART

Use this chart to keep a record of what activities you have completed in this book. Colour in the box next to the activity number and name when it is finished.

Activity number	Page number	Activity name	Completed
1	27	Your differences	
2	28	Your difficulties	
3	29	What I like doing	
4	32	You and ASD	
5	41	Your interests	
6	43	Managing your interests	
7	44	Your interests – problems and benefits	
8	46	Systems, patterns and routines	
9	49	Social skills	
10	52	Communication	
11	55	Sensory issues	
12	64	Family talk	
13	65	Family difficulties	
14	66	House rules	
15	74	Friend checklist	
16	77	Boyfriend or girlfriend checklist	